No Greater Love

Brother Roger of Taizé

No Greater Love

SOURCES OF TAIZÉ

GEOFFREY
CHAPMAN
MOWBRAY

Geoffrey Chapman Mowbray
A Cassell imprint
Wellington House, 125 Strand, London WC2R 0BB, England

Originally published as *Amour de tout amour*,
© Ateliers et Presses de Taizé 1990
Translation © Ateliers et Presses de Taizé 1991

English-language edition first published 1991
Reprinted 1995

British Library Cataloguing in Publication Data
Schutz, Roger
  No greater love.
  1. France. Taizé. Men's religious communities:
  Communauté de Taizé. Roger, of Taizé, Brother
  I. Title   II. Amour de tout amour. *Roger*
  267.23092

ISBN 0–264–67253–4

Cover photographs: Vladimir Sichov, Paris
  Jacques Houzel, *La Vie*, Paris

Typeset by Selectmove Ltd
Printed and bound in Great Britain by
Biddles Ltd, Guildford and King's Lynn

Christ Jesus, you were always within me and I did not realize it. You were there and I was not looking for you.

Having once found you, I longed for you to be the whole of my life. A fire was burning me.

But so often, I began to forget you again. While you kept loving me.

'Someone you do not know is in your midst' (St John).[1]

Wherever you are on the earth, you wish to perceive the mystery that lies at the heart of your heart: do you sense within you, even fleetingly, the silent longing for a presence?

This simple longing, this simple desire for God, is already the beginning of faith.[2]

The One we do not know is in our midst. More accessible for some, more hidden for others . . . with astonishment each of us might hear him say, 'Why be afraid? I, Jesus, am here; I am the Christ. I loved you first[3] . . . in you I have set my joy'.

★　★　★

You know well enough how fragile your response is. Confronted with the absolute challenges of the Gospel, there are times when you feel unprepared.

One of the very first believers already said to Christ, 'I believe; help my unbelief'.[4]

Know once and for all that neither doubts nor the impression that God is silent ever take his Holy Spirit from you.

What God is asking is for you to surrender yourself to Christ in the trust of faith and to welcome his love.

Even though you are pulled in different directions, you alone have to make the choice; no one can make it for you.

Y ou want to follow Christ, and not look back:[5] will
you dare to put your trust in the Gospel time and
time again?[6]

Will you keep setting off anew, drawn on by the One
who walks quietly beside you, never imposing himself?
The Risen Christ is present within you, and goes before
you on the way.

Will you let him place a source of refreshment in the
hollow of your being? Or will you blush with confusion,
and even say: I am not worthy to be loved by him?

What is fascinating about God is how humbly
he is present. God never punishes, never wounds our
human dignity. God does not extort our obedience. Any
authoritarian gesture would disfigure him. The impression

that God comes to punish is one of the greatest obstacles to faith.

Christ, 'poor and humble of heart',[7] never forces anyone's hand.

If he imposed himself, who would dare invite you to follow him?

In the silence of your heart he whispers, 'Don't be afraid; I am here'.[8]

Recognized or not, the Risen Christ remains close to every person, even those unaware of him. He is there in secret.

A fire burning in the human heart, a light in the darkness,[9] he loves you as if you were his sole concern.[10] He has given his life for you.[11] That is his secret.

★   ★   ★

United with Christ, you know that struggle and contemplation have one and the same source. For if you pray, it is because of love; if you struggle to restore their humanity to those mistreated, that too is because of love.

★   ★   ★

Too dazzling to be seen, God seems to blind our sight. But Christ channels this consuming fire and, without dazzling us, allows God to shine through.[12]

Do not be dismayed when the essential seems to remain hidden from your eyes. That only makes you more eager than ever to go on towards the One who is Risen.

Day by day, you will sense more of the depth and the breadth of a love beyond all comprehension.[13] From it, until life's end, you will draw wonder, and also the courage needed for new beginnings.

★   ★   ★

In each person there is a portion of solitude which no human intimacy can ever fill.

Yet you are never alone. Let yourself be plumbed to the depths[14] and you will see that, in your heart of hearts, in the place where no two people are alike, Christ is waiting for you. And what you never dared hope for springs to life.

★   ★   ★

Christ came 'not to abolish but to fulfil'.[15] When you listen, in the silence of your heart, you realize that, far from humiliating human beings, he comes to transfigure even what is most disturbing in you.

Does discovering who you are awaken a kind of inner unrest? But who is going to condemn you when Jesus is praying for you?[16] If you started accusing yourself of all that is in you, would your days and nights be long enough?

When trials arise within you or misunderstandings arrive from without, never forget that in the same wound where the pangs of anxiety are seething, creative forces are also being born. And a way opens up that leads from doubt towards trusting, from dryness to a creation.

★   ★   ★

Are you surrounded by things you cannot understand?
When darkness grows deep, his love is a fire. You need
only fix your gaze on that lamp burning in the darkness,
till day begins to dawn and the sun rises in your heart.[17]

You know very well that you are not the one who
creates this source of light; it comes from Christ.

Dazzling visit of the love of God, the Holy Spirit
flashes through each human life like lightning in the night.
By this mysterious presence, the Risen Christ takes hold
of you; he takes everything upon himself, even the trials so
hard to bear.

Only later, sometimes much later, will you understand
that his overflowing life is never lacking. And you will say,
'Was not my heart burning within me while he spoke to
me?'[18]

★　★　★

Even when you do not recognize him clearly, are you
prepared to remain in the Risen Christ's presence, during
those long periods of silence when nothing seems to be
happening?

There, life's most important decisions take shape.
There, the continual thoughts of 'what's the use?' melt
away.

When you understand little of what he expects
from you, tell him so. In prayer that is humble, tell him
everything, even what you cannot put into words.

Intensely patient, don't worry about not praying
properly. Don't you see that every spiritual pretension
would be like a little death of the soul?

Will you let yourself be drawn to create, by your life, a poem of love with him? Are you prepared to wait for him, the Risen Christ, even when your body and your spirit are like parched and dry ground?

And he elicits in you an intuition, a burst of new energy. . . . Then a desert flower springs up within you, a flower of cheerful joy.[19]

Risen Christ, you take us with our hearts just as they are. Why think we must wait for our hearts to be changed before we go to you? You transfigure them.

With our thorns, you light a fire. The open wound in us is the place through which your love comes streaming. And within the very hurts themselves, you bring to fruition a communion with you.

Your voice comes to rend our night, and the gateways of praise open up within us.

Y ou want to follow Christ, and not look back: remember that, as you walk in his footsteps, you will be irresistibly drawn to share, and to a great simplicity of life.

Perhaps you could place these Gospel words on the wall of your home; they come straight from the heart of Christ: 'Whatever you do to the least of my brothers and sisters, you are doing to me!'[20]

Who will give the best of their creative gifts so that suffering throughout the world may be alleviated, in places where there is sickness or hunger or appalling housing conditions?

Who will understand the cry of all those living in the 'land of the shadow of death'?[21] Who will be a ferment of trust and of peace, so as to break out of a spiral of hatred and fear between individuals and between peoples?

★ ★ ★

Some people wonder: if God existed, surely he would not allow wars, injustice, and the sickness or the oppression of even one single person on earth. If God existed, surely he would keep people from doing wrong.

Nearly three thousand years ago, the prophet Elijah went out into the desert one day to listen to God. A hurricane came roaring by, then an earthquake, then a violent fire. But Elijah realized that God was not in these violent outbursts of nature. Then everything became quiet and Elijah heard God in the murmur of a gentle breeze.[22] And an astonishing fact dawned upon him: often, the voice of God comes to us in a breath of silence.

It was one of the first times in history that this purest of intuitions was written down: God does not terrorize anyone by violent means. God is never the author of evil, of earthquakes, of war or of natural disasters.

Neither suffering nor human distress is willed by God.

God never imposes himself. God leaves us free to love or to hate, to forgive or to refuse forgiveness. But God is never an indifferent witness to human affliction; God suffers with the innocent victim of incomprehensible trials; God suffers with each person.[20] There is a pain that God experiences, a suffering felt by Christ.

★   ★   ★

Are you afraid of your fear? A communion with Christ
gives you the courage needed for a commitment to
make the earth a place fit to live in, so that the most
destitute, those overwhelmed by injustice, are not
forgotten.

Far from submitting passively to the harshest events,
it is possible to use them constructively.

You are not unaware that a fair distribution of wealth
among all is one of the basic conditions for world peace.
And the vast possibilities offered by science and technology
are indispensable in overcoming famine and alleviating
physical suffering.

Are your eyes open to the distress of the innocent,
of all those children scarred by broken relationships,
abandoned by those they love; and also the multitudes
of elderly people who are experiencing unbearable
loneliness?

★ ★ ★

Do not start worrying if you have very little to share: such
weak faith, so few belongings.[23] In the sharing of that
little, God fills your heart to overflowing, inexhaustibly.

Sharing your possessions leads you to simplify your
life and to open your home. So little is needed to welcome
others. Having many possessions is a hindrance rather than
a help to a wider communion. At mealtime, the spirit of
festival flourishes in simplicity.

Simplify in order to live intensely. In so doing you will
discover the joy of being alive.

15

And then, even with very little, your inventive imagination will succeed in creating beauty round about you.

Let a joy sing out within you, at the radiant gift of creation: then your eyes will perceive reflections of eternity.

Christ, Saviour of every life, you come to us always.

Welcoming you in the peace of our nights, in the silence of our days, in the beauty of creation, in the hours of intense inner combat, welcoming you means knowing that you will be with us in every situation, always.

Y ou want to follow Christ, and not look back: are you going to make your way through life with a heart that is reconciled, even amidst the most crippling tensions?

In any disagreement, what is the use of trying to find out who was wrong and who was right?

Suppose people distort your intentions? If you are judged wrongly[24] because of Christ, forgive. You will find that you are free, free beyond compare.

Forgive and then forgive again. That is the highest expression of loving.[25] There you make yours the final prayer of Jesus, 'Forgive them, they do not know what they are doing'.[26]

You forgive, not in order to change the other person, but simply to follow Christ.

Consider your neighbours not just at one particular phase of their existence but through all the stages of their life.

Strive to be transparent. Have nothing to do with clever manoeuvring. Never manipulate another's conscience, using their anxiety as a lever to force them into your way of thinking.

To be free of the Tempter, sing Christ's praises until you are joyful and serene.

His call is to joy, not to despondency.

At every age, forge ahead in faith. Even in days of greyness, his gift of cheerfulness, gaiety even. No lamenting, but at every moment leave everything with him, even your body worn out with fatigue.

* * *

Christ is communion. Will you choose to live a life rooted not in Christ taken in isolation, but in the Risen Lord present on earth in the communion of his Body, his Church? When the Church is a radiant mystery of motherly love and forgiveness, it offers a clear reflection of Christ Jesus.

One of the earliest witnesses to the Gospel had already grasped this: 'Although I might have the gift of speaking in God's name, know all things and have faith strong enough to move mountains, if I do not have love, all that is useless'.[27]

In that unique communion which is the Church, oppositions both ancient and new are tearing the Body of Christ apart.

The luminous ecumenical vocation is and always will be a matter of achieving a reconciliation without delay.

For the Gospel, reconciliation does not wait. 'When you are bringing your gift to the altar and your sister or brother has something against you, leave everything; first go and be reconciled.'[28]

'First go!'. Not, 'Put off till later!'.

Ecumenism fosters illusory hopes when it puts off reconciliation till later. It comes to a standstill, becomes fossilized even, when it accepts the creation of parallel paths on which the vital energies of forgiveness are wasted.

Reconciliation makes us fully consistent with the Gospel . . . and so offers a leaven of peace and trust to the entire human family.

★   ★   ★

But where can we find the fire of a love that reconciles? Where?

As you know, we follow a Christ who 'when overwhelmed by suffering, made no threats against anyone; he bore our sins in his own body, and his wounds have healed us'.[29]

Happy those who, following in his footsteps, go to extremes of compassion. 'Love your enemies, pray for those who are persecuting you.'[30]

If we love only those who love us, we are doing nothing extraordinary. We do not need Christ to do that. A non-believer is quite capable of doing as much.[31]

A conversion takes place in the very depths of our being when, even though we are rejected or humiliated, we entrust to God, at once, those who have wounded us.

*　*　*

Reconciliation is a springtime of the heart. Yes, to become reconciled without delay leads to the amazing discovery that our own hearts are changed by it.

What is to be done if, when you decide to put an end to a break in a relationship, you go and find the people opposing you and tell them, 'I have come to be reconciled', and they reply, 'That is out of the question'?

Will you find the courage to dare once more? Brushing aside the uncertainty that keeps you apart, will you go back to those who have rejected you and say to them, 'I have come to be reconciled'?

And if they send you away again roughly, then – what a discovery! – you find that they have already been welcomed silently within yourself. When you run the risk of trusting, astonishing though it may seem, in you there wells up the incredible lightness of a joy.

*　*　*

In that mystery of communion called the Church, today as in the first century, we are enabled 'with one accord . . . to join constantly in prayer . . . with Mary, the mother of Jesus'.[32]

And the Virgin Mary sheds light on our ways. In her, a catholicity of heart. Her song wells up in the Magnificat: she dares to hope for everyone. In a prophetic vision, she foresees that through the coming of her Son a source of salvation for all people has appeared.[33]

In Mary, motherly love and catholicity are one and the same. Is this not true of the Church as well? When one of these realities grows weak, the other gradually fades away.

★   ★   ★

Filled with the Holy Spirit, century after century Christians have communicated to others the trust of faith.

And are you going to be someone who will open up the ways of the Risen Christ?[34] Or will you hesitate and say, 'Why do you ask me to prepare ways of the Gospel for others? Can't you see that I am quite helpless, like a child?'

Who can tell all that certain children communicate through gifts they are still unaware of?[35] Some of them awaken others to God by the trust they display, by unexpected words.

You awaken others to Christ above all by the life you lead. Words alone can easily make do with illusions. When a small-group discussion turns into mere chatter about God, the Holy Spirit, or communion with Christ, is there still anything creative about it?

You communicate the life of the Risen Christ through a profound personal unselfishness, by forgetting about yourself.

Instead of short-lived outbursts of enthusiasm, will you fashion for yourself a steadfast heart so as to be faithful to the end?[36]

Christ Jesus, even if we had faith enough to move mountains, without living charity,[27] *what would we be?*

You love us.

Without your Holy Spirit who lives in our hearts,[37] *what would we be?*

You love us.

Taking everything upon yourself, you open for us a way towards faith, towards trust in God, who wants neither suffering nor human distress.

Spirit of the Risen Christ, Spirit of compassion, Spirit of praise, your love for each one of us will never disappear.[38]

W ho will make level for you the paths leading to the fountains of living water? There, and only there, the vital energy needed for risk-taking comes flowing.

You ask yourself: 'How can I find fulfilment?' You are not interested in a settled life, with no risks; you long to make something of your life.

Waste no time in dead-end situations; you would be using up vital energy. No self-indulgence. Move on, without a moment's hesitation. Your heart will grow wider as you discover that our life finds fulfilment only in the presence of God.

You say to yourself: how can I find fulfilment when images from the past or present-day situations cover the wellsprings and awaken clinging regret?

Never forget: God takes care of all your cares.

And even when the meaning of life gets lost, a spark of light blazes up. It lights up your night. His love is a fire . . .

. . . The fire of his forgiveness flames deep within you, dispelling your own confusion. He calls you by name.[39] That fire burns the very roots of bitterness. That fire never says 'enough'.[40]

★ ★ ★

Fulfilment? Are you hesitating over a choice for fear of making a mistake?

Stop summoning your own darkness to cover your confusion. Happy all those who tear their hands from their eyes and dare to go forward, sustained solely by the trusting of faith.[41]

Fulfilment? Become what you are in your heart of hearts . . .

. . . and the gates of a spirit of childhood will open, the wonder of a love.

A fountain of gladness surges up for you. Not euphoria, not just any kind of joy, but the jubilation that comes straight from the wellsprings of eternity.

★ ★ ★

If the spirit of festivity were to fade away. . . .

If we were to wake up, one fine morning, in a society that was functional, technologically advanced, but where all inner life had vanished. . . .

Science and technology are indispensable for making the earth fit to live in. But if we forgot the trust of faith and the intelligence of the heart, so vital in building the future of the human family. . . .

Where could we find an overflowing inner life, if the spirit of joy vanished from that unique communion which is the Body of Christ, his Church, and if the Church's motherly love were replaced by moralistic speeches?

If we were to lose childlike trust in the Eucharist and in the Word of God. . . .

If the prayer of Christians were expressed in a language heavy with boredom, leaving no room for intuition, for poetry, for the adorable presence of the Risen Christ. . . .

Jesus, Risen Lord, at times you see me bewildered, like a stranger on this earth. But a thirst fills my soul, the longing for your presence. And my heart finds no rest until it can lay in you, Christ, what was weighing it down and keeping it far from you.

I f everything began with a heart that trusts, who could still say, 'What am I doing on this earth?'

For trust to rise up all across the world, in the East and the West, in the North and the South, your life and the lives of a great many people are necessary.[42]

If a passion for forgiveness were ablaze within you, then you could kindle sparks of communion even in the darkest days of nations.

The experience of a whole lifetime is not necessary in order to begin.

Do not forget that, in the most difficult periods of history, very often a small number of women, men and young people, and even children, spread out over the earth, were able to change the course of certain historical developments. Persevering in communion with Christ Jesus in prayerful waiting or in a life of contemplation, they were an invisible ferment of reconciliation among believers and non-believers.

At present, too, there are people who have all they need to transform situations that have become rigid. Leaving behind the age of mistrust, or even suspicion, they have all they need to create an era of trust and of reconciliations.

Eagerly longing for divisions to be healed, they stand in the midst of humanity as signs of what we could never have hoped for.

They can be recognized. They have been fashioned by times of inconceivable trial. They persevere in spite of everything,[43] in spite of all that cannot be changed.

By the gift of their lives, they show that human beings were not created for hopelessness.

For them, although there are walls to be demolished, there is above all a 'unique source' where the courage for new beginnings can be found again and again.

★   ★   ★

How can we discover that 'unique source', where the Gospel appears in all its first freshness?

You may have already noticed that, in the innermost depths of the human condition, there lies the longing for a presence.

Remember, the simple desire for God is already the beginning of faith.[2]

And when Jesus the Christ allows himself to be perceived in the beauty of an inclusive common prayer, the thirst to understand grows more intense.

At the outset, extensive knowledge is not what matters. That has great value. But it is first of all by intuition that you penetrate the Mystery of Faith. Knowledge will come later. Everything is not given at one time.

*   *   *

If Jesus had not come to earth, God might still seem far off, and even out of reach. Christ, the Risen Lord, makes God accessible to our lives.[12]

Will you always remember this luminous Gospel reality: 'We are not the ones who loved God; God loved us first'?[3] That is a light for your life.

However inconceivable it may seem, as you surrender yourself to him, do not worry if you do not manage to love him immediately.

*   *   *

In the Gospel, Jesus assures you that, by worrying, you can do nothing.[44] You have to accept your limitations and what is fragile in you.

Why dwell on what hurts, both in yourself and in others?

You know the words of one of the first witnesses to Christ, 'Even if our hearts condemn us, God is greater than our hearts'.[45]

Jesus the Christ does not invite you to be preoccupied with yourself, but to a humble repentance of heart. What does that mean? It is that movement of trust whereby you cast your faults on him. And there you are, released, even liberated, ready to live the present moment intensely, never discouraged because always forgiven.

Perhaps you say, 'That's not possible'?

Christ also offers you his compassion in the sacrament of reconciliation. And you will grasp that, even though you may experience trials, your life is woven through with the threads of his forgiveness.

*   *   *

The Risen Christ is close to you. 'His Kingdom is within us.'[46] And within you rises up a kind of inner voice, and that voice is prayer. Although your lips remain closed, your silent heart is listening, wide open in the presence of God.

When you pray with words, they are sometimes poor and awkward. You tell God your joys and your disappointments, everything. When you pray alone, the language you use is of little importance. It will not disconcert or offend other people.

And Christ challenges you through events. He suggests an intuition, and then it rises up within you and works on you. Even if you only retain one word of it, that word can open up a way forward.

In you, this prayer:

'Saviour of every life, the days went by and I did not respond to you. I went so far as to wonder whether I really needed God at all. Walls of hesitation and doubt had risen up and made me drift far from you.

'Jesus Christ, mysterious Presence, you were waiting for me. In the depths of my contradictions, and even of my inner revolts, I perceived a luminous Gospel insight: your love is not an empty word; it is your continual presence; it is your forgiveness.

'By the Holy Spirit, you, the Risen Lord, were living in me and you had never left me.'[47]

*   *   *

When Christ asks you, 'For you, who am I?',[48] suppose you were to reply:

'Christ Jesus, you are the One who loves me into the life that has no end.

'You open for me the way of risk. You are expecting from me not just a few crumbs, but the whole of my existence.

'You are praying within me, day and night.[49] My stammerings are prayer: simply calling you by the Name of Jesus fills the empty places in my heart.

'You place on my finger the ring of the prodigal son, the ring of festival.[50]

'And for my part, did I "exchange the radiance of God for half-heartedness? Did I abandon the source of living water and dig myself cracked cisterns that hold no water?"[51]

'Christ, tirelessly you were seeking me.

'Why did I hesitate, asking for time to look after my own affairs? Once I had put my hand to the plough, why did I look back?'

'And yet, though I had never seen you, I loved you, perhaps not as I would have liked to, but I did love you.[52]

'Christ Jesus, you were suggesting to me, "Live the very little of the Gospel that you have understood; proclaim my life among humanity; come and follow me".[53]

'Until one day, returning to the source, I understood. You were asking me to commit myself to the point of no return.'

THE 'LITTLE SOURCE' OF TAIZÉ

For the Taizé Community, the 'little source'
expresses the essential which makes a common
life possible.

D esiring as you do to give your life because of Christ
and the Gospel,[1] always keep in mind that you are
advancing with him towards the light, even in the midst of
your own darkness.

So, no longer looking back,[2] run forward in the
footsteps of Jesus the Christ. He is leading you along
a path of light: I am, but also, you are the light of the
world.[3]

You wish to prepare the ways of the Lord Christ for
many others,[4] kindling a fire even in the world's darkest
nights.[5]

You know that Jesus the Christ came for all,[6] not
just for a few. Risen, he is united with every human being

without exception. Such is the catholicity of heart God
has set within you.

Will you let an inner life, that has neither beginning
nor end, grow within you? There, you stand at the
threshold of the Gospel's joy, where human solidarities
plunge their roots.

*　　*　　*

Making the earth a place where all can live, be they nearby
or far away, is one of the beautiful pages of the Gospel for
you to write by your life.

By forgetting yourself, by not seeking your own
advantage, you are enabled to stand firm in the midst of
the human family's situations, with all their constant ebb
and flow. Will you seek to understand, without letting
yourself be carried away by the successive waves?

By sharing, are you among those who, with very little,
give rise to a fine human hope on earth?

With almost nothing, are you a creator of reconciliation in that mystery of communion which is the
Church?

Sustained by a shared momentum, rejoice: you are
no longer alone; in all things you are advancing together
with your brothers. With them, you are called to live a
parable of community.

A lthough perhaps you sense no echo of it, Christ's mysterious presence never forsakes you. The impression of doubt can at times seem to exist within you, but there is above all the miracle of his continual presence.

Sometimes you suddenly find yourself asking him, 'What are you expecting of me?'

And you say to the Risen Christ, 'Listen, listen to my child's prayer and enable me to entrust everything to you at every moment'.

★　★　★

God could do without our prayer. It is a mystery that he sets such store by it.

God understands every human language. Remaining close to him in silence is already prayer: your lips remain closed but your heart is speaking to him. And, by the Holy Spirit, Christ prays in you more than you imagine.[7]

In the common prayer, the spirit of praise gives glimpses of the invisible. In it you receive a kind of 'shock of meaning'. And within you comes welling up the wonder of a love.

Don't worry if your attention sometimes wanders during the common prayer. Your mere presence is itself already an expression of your longing for the living God; it is a prelude to contemplation.

*   *   *

Throughout your day, work and rest are enlivened by the Word of God.

Mindful of the age-old prayer 'praised be the Lord and I am set free from the enemy',[8] dare to say to the Tempter, 'I don't have one second of my life to give you!'

Christ offers himself in the Eucharist. Adorable presence, the Eucharist is there for you who are poor and in need.

I f a heart that trusts were at the beginning
of everything. . . .

Trust in God, faith, is such a simple reality, so simple
that everyone can welcome it. It is a kind of reawakening
repeated time and time again.

Remember this once and for all: God never imposes
himself by dictates and threats. Christ never wishes anyone
to suffer torment. If, for you, a life in God were to mean
being afraid of God, you should think again.

God is love, and love alone.[9] The will of his love is not
some kind of law harshly chiselled on tables of stone. By
the Holy Spirit, it is written deep in the human heart.[10]

One day you understood that, without your being aware of it, a yes had already been inscribed in your innermost depths. And so you chose to go forward in the footsteps of Christ, a choice no one can make for another.

In silence in the presence of Christ, you heard him say, 'Come, follow me;[11] I will give you a place to rest your heart'.

And so you are led to the audacity of a yes that lasts until your dying breath. This yes leaves you exposed. There is no other way.

★　★　★

Christ could say to you:

'I have shared everything. I have experienced the goodness and the generosity of the human heart. I encountered the Tempter more than once. I have also known what it means to be forsaken by those close to me. After having been my companions, some abandoned me.

'And I asked some of the others, "Do you want to leave me too?"[12] You think you have nothing, or almost nothing, with which to respond to me by a yes for your entire lifetime. I am familiar with your trials and your poverty, yet you are filled to the full.'[13]

★　★　★

That yes keeps you alert. What was incomplete, and even the element of human error it might have contained at the outset, are consumed in the fire of Christ's love.

Only let the flame that never dies away keep burning. And the yes blazes up within.

The yes of celibacy is accomplished in the giving of one's life . . . and it becomes possible again and again to go beyond oneself. The heart, the affections, the solitude are all still there, but someone Other than oneself is transfiguring them.

And your soul can sing: I belong to Christ, I am Christ's.

★   ★   ★

The prior, as servant of communion, seeks to make his brothers attentive to living all together a parable of communion.

He should not consider himself as being above his brothers but, as he fixes the orientations of the community without being bound by a majority, let him seek to understand in God the will of his love.

If he senses a lack of agreement on an important question, he indicates a provisional direction, ready to review it later.

Discernment, the spirit of mercy and an inexhaustible goodness of heart are irreplaceable gifts for him.

He designates a brother to ensure continuity after him.

★   ★   ★

During the council, we prepare ourselves together in inner silence, as Christ's poor, to discover a Gospel freshness in our common calling.

'Eager for the gifts of the Spirit, we are seeking to be filled with them, so as to build up the community.'[14]

Nothing would be as paralysing as authoritarian 'we musts'. Discussions about everything do not build up a common life. How could men advancing towards Christ keep moving ahead if they got bogged down in quagmires of indecision?

   ★ ★ ★

Every meal can be a time when a brotherly communion finds expression.

At table, times of silence bring peace of heart.

The simplicity of the food reminds us that we have chosen a way that involves sharing with those most in need.[15]

   ★ ★ ★

The new brothers need time to mature, in order to understand the vocation in all its consequences.

Certain brothers have been given the responsibility of listening to them and of preparing them for the yes of a whole lifetime.

   ★ ★ ★

Brothers in far-off places are called to be signs of Christ and bearers of joy.

Wherever they live, the eucharistic presence can turn even the poorest of dwellings into a place that is inhabited.

When you share the living conditions of the poor, are you sufficiently aware that, through your mere presence, God transfigures something of the trials of the human family?

Wherever you are, you carry within you one and the same calling. It is up to you always to be careful that your life reflects the vocation of our whole community.

* * *

Will the people we welcome day after day find in us men radiant with Christ, our peace?

It is most essential that the hospitality we are called to offer to so many be carried out in a spirit of discernment. Any over-familiarity would obscure the meaning of our vocation.

Certain brothers, gifted with discernment, are appointed to listen to those who come with something to confide. They listen not primarily to give advice, but to prepare the ways of the Lord Christ in those who come:[16] are they sufficiently aware of all their inner resources, of all the gifts placed within them?

* * *

Your life is rooted in a community, itself a part of the Church. Consequently you can pray:

Jesus, my joy, my hope and my life, look not on my sins but on the faith, the trust, of your Church.

In the footsteps of the witnesses of all the ages, from Mary and the apostles down to believers of the present day, enable me to dispose myself, in an inner life, to put my trust in the Mystery of Faith.[17]

T he peace of your heart makes life beautiful for those
around you.

Being wracked with worry has never been a way of
living the Gospel. Founding your faith on torment would
mean building a house on sand.[18]

Each day, do you hear these words of Jesus the Christ,
'Peace I leave you; my peace I give you. Let your hearts
cease to be troubled and afraid'?[19]

Peace in the depths permits you to set out again, when
failure or discouragements weigh on your shoulders.

And sheer wonder comes alive, along with a breath of
poetry, a simplicity of life and, for those able to understand
it, a mystical vision of the human person.

For you this Gospel prayer:

Bless us, Lord Christ; bless us and those you have entrusted to us. Keep us in the spirit of the Beatitudes,[20]
   joy,
   simplicity,
   mercy.

P eace of heart is a mainstay of the inner life; it sustains us as we make our way upward towards joy.

Peace and joy are Gospel pearls. They come to fill chasms of anxiety.

Will you welcome each new day as God's today? In every season, will you find ways of discovering life's poetry, on days full of light as in winter's frozen nights? Will you discover how to bring joy to your humble dwelling by small signs that cheer the heart?

The presence of the Risen Christ leads to unexpected moments of happiness; it breaks through your nights. 'Darkness is not darkness with you; the night shines bright as day.'[21]

★　　★　　★

You are called to freedom.[22] Your past is buried in the heart of Christ, and God has already taken care of your future.

Do not be afraid of suffering. In the very depths of the abyss, a perfection of joy can be found in communion with Christ Jesus.

Dare to rejoice in what God is accomplishing through you and around you. Then all forms of pessimism about yourself and about others, which were waging war on your soul, will melt away.

If you forgot the gifts of the Holy Spirit[23] in you, and you lost the last traces of self-esteem, then what a risk of losing your balance. . .! The void attracts, fascinates.

With joy comes a sense of wonder. Such a joy needs nothing less than our whole being in order to shine forth. It lies in the transparent openness of peaceful love.

Unless the grain of wheat dies.[24] . . . Paschal joy, the joy of Easter, brings healing to the secret wounds of the soul. It does not make the heart proud. It can do without applause. It goes straight to the gateways of light.

Spirit of the Risen Christ, mysterious Presence, enable us so to root our lives in your trust, that the wellsprings of jubilation never run dry.

'Sell what you have, give it to the poor, then come, follow me.'[25] This challenge of Christ Jesus is one of the most astonishing in the Gospel.

Our vocation as community has committed us to live solely from our work, accepting neither donations nor bequests nor gifts – nothing, absolutely nothing.

The boldness involved in not ensuring any capital for ourselves, without fear of possible poverty, is a source of incalculable strength.

The spirit of poverty does not consist in looking poverty-stricken, but in arranging everything with imagination, in creation's simple beauty.

Happy all who love simplicity: in them is the Kingdom of God.[26]

A constant simplifying of our existence keeps us far from those tortuous paths where we go astray.

Simplicity devoid of burning charity is a shadow without light. If a great simplicity of life were full of bitterness and laden with judgements, then where would be the joyfulness of each present day?

* * *

Sunlight breaking suddenly through the clouds: when the energies of the prime of life combine in you with the spirit of childhood, your soul draws near to serene joy.

Creator Spirit, you clothe the flowers of the field:[27] *grant us to rejoice in all that you pour out upon us, and may that be enough for us.*

I f you were to lose mercy, the heart's compassion, you would have lost everything.

Will you let yourself be challenged by that absolute of love, the call to forgive even seventy times seven times, in other words always?[28]

With lightened step, you will go forward from one discovery to another.

For those who love, and forget themselves, life is filled with serene beauty. All friendship involves an inner struggle. And sometimes the cross comes to illuminate the unfathomable depth of loving.

Rather than trying to impose yourself by creating a bad conscience around you, or slipping into an ironic tone, will you let yourself overflow with kindness?

In the transparency of this loving, admit your mistakes simply and do not waste time looking at the speck in your brother's eye.[29]

Happy the community which becomes an abyss of kindness: it lets Christ shine through, incomparably.

★　★　★

Christ, love of all loving, is a fire that burns within you. And when love is forgiveness, your heart, though tested, begins to live once more.

The contemplation of his forgiveness becomes a radiant kindness in hearts that are simple. And the holiness of Christ is no longer out of reach.

We know him so little, but he is in our midst[30] . . . and there comes a breath that will never die away . . . and that little is enough for us.

Do not be afraid, trust is at hand, and with it a happiness.

Christ Jesus, inner Light, enable me to welcome your presence, that I may know joy.

I love you, perhaps not as I would like to, but I do love you. . . .

Love of all loving, you know that I will give my very life for you and your Gospel.

THE LIFE COMMITMENT

The following words are spoken on the day
a brother makes his life commitment
in the Taizé Community.

B ROTHER, what do you ask?

The mercy of God and the community of my brothers.

May God complete in you what he has begun.

Brother, you trust in God's mercy: remember that the Lord Christ comes to help the weakness of your faith; committing himself with you, he fulfils for you his promise:

'Truly, there is no one who has given up home, brothers, sisters, mother, father, wife or children for my sake and the Gospel's, who will not receive a hundred times as much at present – homes and brothers and sisters and mothers and children – and persecutions too, and in the age to come eternal life.'[1]

This is a way contrary to all human reason; like Abraham you can only advance along it by faith, not by sight,[2] always sure that whoever loses his life for Christ's sake will find it.[3]

From now on walk in the steps of Christ. Do not be anxious about tomorrow.[4] First seek God's Kingdom and its justice.[5] Surrender yourself, give yourself, and good measure, pressed down, shaken together, brimming over, will be poured out for you; the measure you give is the measure you will receive.[6]

Whether you wake or sleep, night and day the seed springs up and grows, you do not know how.[7]

Avoid parading your goodness before people to gain their admiration.[8] Never let your inner life make you look sad, like a hypocrite who puts on a grief-stricken air to attract attention. Anoint your head and wash your face, so that only your Father who is in secret knows what your heart intends.[9]

Stay simple and full of joy, the joy of the merciful, the joy of brotherly love.

Be vigilant. If you have to rebuke a brother, keep it between the two of you.[10]

Be concerned to establish communion with your neighbour.

Be open about yourself, remembering that you have a brother whose charge it is to listen to you. Bring him your understanding so that he can fulfil his ministry with joy.[11]

The Lord Christ, in his compassion and his love for you, has chosen you to be in the Church a sign of brotherly love. It is his will that with your brothers you live the parable of community.

So, refusing to look back,[12] and joyful with infinite gratitude, never fear to rise to meet the dawn,[13]

praising
blessing
and singing
Christ your Lord.

Receive me, Lord, and I will live; may my expectation be a source of joy.

Brother, remember that it is Christ who calls you and that it is to him that you are now going to respond.

Will you, for love of Christ, consecrate yourself to him with all your being?
I will.
Will you henceforth fulfil your service of God within our community, in communion with your brothers?
I will.
Will you, renouncing all ownership, live with your brothers not only in community of material goods but also in community of spiritual goods, striving for openness of heart?
I will.
Will you, in order to be more available to serve with your brothers, and in order to give yourself in undivided love to Christ, remain in celibacy?
I will.
Will you, so that we may be of one heart and one mind and so that the unity of our common service may be fully achieved, adopt the orientations of the community expressed by the prior, bearing in mind that he is only a poor servant in the community?
I will.
Will you, always discerning Christ in your brothers, watch over them in good days and bad, in suffering and in joy?
I will.
In consequence, because of Christ and the Gospel, you are henceforth a brother of our community.

May this ring be the sign of our fidelity in the Lord.

Within me my soul is thirst-ing:
to sur-ren-der all in you, O Christ.
And my heart with-in is ev-er yearn-ing,
un-til it finds rest in you.

Words by Brother Roger
© Presses de Taizé
Music: J.S. BACH

WORDS OF
JOHN PAUL II
IN TAIZÉ

P ope *John Paul II visited the Taizé Community on 5 October 1986. During the common prayer, the Pope explained to the young people gathered in Taizé the meaning of his visit:*

One passes through Taizé as one passes close to a spring of water. The traveller stops, quenches his thirst and continues on his way. The brothers of the community, you know, do not want to keep you. They want, in prayer and silence, to enable you to drink the living water promised by Christ, to know his joy, to discern his presence, to respond to his call, then to set out again to witness to his love and to serve your brothers and sisters in your parishes, your schools, your universities, and in all your places of work.

Today in all the Churches and Christian communities, and even among the highest political leaders in the world, the Taizé Community is known for the trust always full of hope that it places in the young. It is above all because I share this trust and this hope that I have come here this morning.

After the common prayer, John Paul II met with the brothers of the community:

Dear brothers, in the family-like intimacy of this brief meeting, I would like to express to you my affection and my trust with these simple words, with which Pope John XXIII, who loved you so much, greeted Brother Roger one day: 'Ah, Taizé, that little springtime!'

My desire is that the Lord may keep you like a springtime that blossoms and that he keep you little, in the joy of the Gospel and the transparency of brotherly love.

Each of you came here to live in the mercy of God and the community of his brothers. In consecrating your whole being to Christ for love of him, you found both of these.

But in addition, although you did not look for it, you have seen young people from everywhere come to you by the thousands, attracted by your prayer and your community life. How can we not think that these young people are the gift and the means the Lord gives you to stimulate you to remain together, in the joy and the freshness of your gift, as a springtime for all who are searching for true life?

Throughout your days, work, rest, prayer, everything is enlivened by the Word of God that takes hold of you, that keeps you little, in other words children of the heavenly Father, brothers and servants of all in the joy of the Beatitudes.

I do not forget that in its unique, original and in a certain sense provisional vocation, your community can awaken astonishment and encounter incomprehension and suspicion. But because of your passion for the reconciliation of all Christians in a full communion, because of your love for the Church, you will be able to continue, I am sure, to be open to the will of the Lord.

By listening to the criticisms or suggestions of Christians of different Churches and Christian communities and keeping what is good, by remaining in dialogue with all but not hesitating to express your expectations and your projects, you will not disappoint the young, and you will be instrumental in making sure that the effort desired by Christ to recover the visible unity of his Body in the full communion of one and the same faith never slackens. You know how much I personally consider ecumenism a necessity incumbent upon me, a pastoral priority in my ministry for which I count on your prayer.

By desiring to be yourselves a 'parable of community', you will help all you meet to be faithful to their church affiliation, the fruit of their education and their choice in conscience, but also to enter more and more deeply into the mystery of communion that the Church is in God's plan.

By his Gift to his Church, Christ liberates in every Christian forces of love and gives them a universal heart to be creators of justice and peace, able to unite to their contemplation a struggle along the lines of the Gospel for the integral liberation of human beings, of every human being and of the entire human being.

Dear brothers, I thank you for having invited me and thus having given me the opportunity to return to Taizé. May the Lord bless you and keep you in his peace and his love!

Notes

1. John 1.26
2. Luke 17.5–6
3. 1 John 4.10, 19
4. Mark 9.24
5. Luke 9.62
6. Mark 1.15
7. Matthew 11.29
8. Matthew 14.27
9. John 1.4–5
10. Isaiah 43.4
11. John 15.13
12. John 1.18
13. Ephesians 3.18–19
14. Romans 8.27
15. Matthew 5.17
16. Romans 8.34
17. 2 Peter 1.19
18. Luke 24.32
19. Isaiah 35.1–2
20. Matthew 25.40
21. Isaiah 9.1 and Luke 1.79
22. 1 Kings 19.9–13
23. Luke 21.1–4
24. Matthew 5.11–12
25. Matthew 18.21–22
26. Luke 23.34
27. 1 Corinthians 13.2
28. Matthew 5.23–24
29. 1 Peter 2.23–24
30. Luke 6.27–28
31. Luke 6.32–34
32. Acts 1.14
33. Luke 1.46–55
34. Matthew 3.3
35. See Luke 9.46–48
36. See Revelation 2.9–10 and Sirach 2.2
37. Ezekiel 36.27
38. Isaiah 54.10

39. John 10.3
40. Proverbs 30.16
41. Hebrews 11.8
42. Hebrews 12.1
43. See Romans 4.18
44. Luke 12.25–26
45. 1 John 3.20
46. Luke 17.21

47. See Galatians 2.20
48. Matthew 16.15
49. See Mark 4.27
50. Luke 15.22–24
51. Jeremiah 2.13
52. 1 Peter 1.8
53. John 21.22

The 'Little Source' of Taizé

1. Mark 10.29 and Matthew 16.25
2. Luke 9.62
3. John 8.12 and Matthew 5.14
4. Mark 1.3
5. Luke 12.49
6. Titus 2.11
7. Romans 8.26
8. Psalm 18.3
9. 1 John 4.16
10. Jeremiah 31.33 and 2 Corinthians 3.3
11. Mark 10.21
12. John 6.67
13. Revelation 2.9

14. 1 Corinthians 14.12
15. See Matthew 25.34–40
16. John 1.23
17. See 1 Tim 3.9, 15–16
18. Matthew 7.26–27
19. John 14.27
20. See Matthew 5.3–12
21. Psalm 139.12
22. Galatians 5.13
23. 2 Timothy 1.6–7
24. John 12.24
25. Matthew 19.21
26. Matthew 5.3
27. Matthew 6.28–29
28. Matthew 18.21–22
29. Matthew 7.3–5
30. John 1.26

The Life Commitment

1. Mark 10.29–30 and Luke 18.29–30
2. 2 Corinthians 5.7
3. Matthew 16.25
4. Matthew 6.34
5. Matthew 6.33
6. Luke 6.38

7. Mark 4.27
8. Matthew 6.1
9. Matthew 6.16–18
10. Matthew 18.15
11. Hebrews 13.17
12. Philippians 3.13
13. Psalm 119.147

The Story of Taizé

BROTHER ROGER founded the Taizé Community as an attempt to find ways beyond divisions between Christians and conflicts in the human family. Today, Taizé is a place where hundreds of thousands of young adults from every continent come to pray and to prepare themselves to work for peace, reconciliation and trust in the world.

The Beginnings

When the founder of Taizé is asked about the early influences that shaped his life, he often replies by speaking about his grandmother. During World War I, she was a widow, living in the North of France. Her three sons were fighting on the front lines. Even when the bombs were falling nearby, she remained at home in order to welcome refugees – old people, little children, pregnant women. She left only at the very last minute, when everybody had to flee. Her one desire was that no one else would ever have to go through what she had experienced. Christians, divided among themselves, had been killing one another in Europe; at least they should be reconciled, she said, to help prevent another war. She came from a family that had been Protestant for generations. To make reconciliation a reality already within herself, she went to the Catholic church, without it being seen as a repudiation of her own people.

These two aspirations of his grandmother – taking risks for those most in need at the time, and becoming reconciled with the Catholic faith – marked Brother Roger for life.

In 1940, when he was twenty-five, another war broke out. For several years already he had been thinking about creating a monastic community devoted to reconciliation. He left Switzerland, his country of birth, and settled in Burgundy, France, the land of his mother, to be present in the midst of war and suffering. 'The more a believer wishes to live the absolute call of God', he would later write, 'the more essential it is to do so in the heart of human distress.'

Looking for a house, he arrived in the town of Cluny, which he knew because of its role in the history of monasticism. Nearby he found a house for sale in the village of Taizé. An old woman welcomed him, and when he told her of his plan, she said, 'Stay here; we are so isolated'. He saw this as God's voice speaking to him through a poor woman. He had heard no such words in any of the other places he had visited.

Taizé was two kilometres from the line of demarcation which at that time divided France in two. In the house he purchased, he hid political refugees, mostly Jews, who were fleeing from the Nazi-occupied zone. He remained in Taizé from 1940 to 1942. Alone, he prayed three times a day in a tiny oratory, just as the community whose creation he was meditating would later do. When the Gestapo made several visits to his house, he was forced to leave France from late 1942 to the end of 1944.

A 'Parable of Communion'

In 1944, when he returned to Taizé, Brother Roger was accompanied by his first three brothers, whom he had met in the meantime. In 1949, the first seven brothers made lifetime monastic commitments: celibacy, acceptance of the ministry of the prior, community of material and spiritual goods. Brother Roger was the prior. In 1952, he wrote the first version of the 'Rule of Taizé'; from its title onwards, it would be constantly revised in the course of the years and become, for the fiftieth anniversary of Taizé in 1990, the heart of the book *No Greater Love: Sources of Taizé*.

From the beginning, the community took its place as part of the great monastic family. Taizé is ten kilometres from Cluny, that ancient monastic centre, and not far from Cîteaux, another important monastery of the past. Later on Brother Roger would see a symbolic meaning in this fact: 'Taizé is like a bud grafted on the tree of monastic life. It is undoubtedly significant that our village lies between Cluny and Cîteaux. On the one hand there is Cluny, with its humanness, its sense of moderation and of continuities. Cluny, the centre of attraction for so many Christians seeking their own inner unity and unity with their neighbours. On the other hand there is Cîteaux, revitalized by St Bernard with reforming zeal and a refusal to compromise the absolute of the Gospel, with a sense of the demands of the present moment. In their footsteps, we would like to fuse a sense of urgency with a sense of long continuities.'

The Taizé Community grew as the years passed. In 1969, Catholic brothers were able to enter. Today there are 90 brothers, Catholics and from different Protestant backgrounds, from some twenty different countries.

By its very existence, the community is a sign of reconciliation among divided Christians, among separated peoples. It forms what Brother Roger refers to as a 'parable of communion'.

Reconciliation between Christians is at the heart of Taizé's calling, but this is never seen as an end in itself; it is so that Christians may be a ferment of reconciliation, of trust among nations, of peace on earth.

The community accepts no gifts or donations for its own life. The brothers do not even accept personal inheritances. They support themselves and others by their work.

As soon as the community numbered twelve brothers, in the 1950s, some of them went to live outside Taizé, to be witnesses of peace in the midst of division and to share the life of the victims of poverty. Today, there are brothers living in poor areas of North and South America, Asia and Africa. They share the living conditions of those around them; they listen to them and support those who are looking for local solutions to their problems.

Periodically, Brother Roger goes to spend time in places undergoing difficulties, to be close to those suffering trials and sometimes to increase people's awareness of a situation. He has stayed several times with his brothers in 'Hell's Kitchen', a section of New York City where many minorities live. He went to Chile after the *coup d'état* there. He has also stayed in a poor neighbourhood of Calcutta, in South Africa, in the region of a serious earthquake in the South of Italy, in Lebanon, in Haiti, in sub-Saharan Africa suffering from drought, in a poor district of Madras and in Ethiopia. Each year he goes to Eastern Europe where, since the early 1960s, the community has had long-term relationships with Christians of all ages.

Taizé and the young: the Intercontinental Meetings

Since 1957–58, Taizé has welcomed young adults in ever greater numbers. They come from Portugal as well as Sweden, from Scotland as well as Poland, and from other continents too, to take part in week-long meetings centred on the wellsprings of faith. Despite the divisions in Europe, the number of young people from the East has grown steadily, and this was true quite a while before the opening of the borders in 1989. Today, faces and clothing from a great variety of human backgrounds are visible on the hill of Taizé. In the space of a year, young adults of almost a hundred different nationalities pass through Taizé to participate in the intercontinental meetings there. Many families come with small children, too, to spend a week meeting with families from other lands. Without counting the thousands of pilgrims who pass through Taizé each day for a few hours, these intercontinental meetings bring together up to 6,000 young people a week in the summer, and between 500 and 1,000 in the spring and autumn. Easter, Pentecost and All Saints' are the times when visitors are most numerous.

The travel costs of those coming from the southern continents are taken care of by parishes in Europe. After a time of preparation in Taizé, the young people from other continents spend a few weeks visiting these parishes. For centuries, it was above all from Europe that the Gospel was brought to the rest of the world. Today these young people, who often come from countries where faith is more alive, are taking part in a new evangelization of Europe, in the birth of a springtime of the Church.

Over the years, hundreds of thousands of young people searching for meaning in their life have come to Taizé. They have reflected on the link between faith and commitment, between inner life and human solidarities. Several generations have acquired not only a deeper understanding of prayer and a more universal vision of the Church, but also a concern for human rights, an international awareness, a trust in foreigners and a greater attention to peace and sharing between cultures.

Three times each day, everyone goes to the 'Church of Reconciliation' for the common prayer. Built in 1962, the church has often had to be extended by large tents; in 1990, a large narthex was added. The 'songs of Taizé' are easily recognizable: composed in many different languages, they are made up of a simple phrase sung over and over again, as a way of expressing a basic reality, quickly grasped by the mind and then gradually penetrating one's entire being. After the evening prayer, brothers remain in the church to listen to those who wish to express a personal problem or question.

Every Saturday evening a prayer of Ressurrection is celebrated, a festival of light. And it was from Moscow that Brother Roger brought back the following symbol: every Friday evening the icon of the Cross is placed in the centre of the Church; people come and pray around it in silence as a way of entrusting to God their own burdens and those of others, as a way of joining the Risen Christ who remains alongside all who are undergoing trials.

Since 1966, the Sisters of St Andrew, an international Catholic community founded 750 years ago, have been living in a neighbouring village. They assume part of the responsibility for welcoming people to Taizé.

A Pilgrimage of Trust on Earth

In 1970, Brother Roger launched the idea of a 'council of youth'; its main gathering took place in 1974. At a time when young people were experiencing discouragement and leaving the churches, the Council of Youth offered them a hope of taking part in the reconciliation of Christians and the creation of peace on earth. Set aside temporarily in 1979 until the moment would arrive for it to be taken up again, the Council of Youth laid the groundwork for a pilgrimage of reconciliation across the earth.

In 1982, during a stay in Lebanon, Brother Roger proposed the idea of a 'pilgrimage of trust on earth'. Young and old were invited not to join a movement centred on Taizé, but to become, in their own situations, pilgrims of peace, bearers of reconciliation in the Church and of trust on earth, by becoming involved in their neighbourhoods, in their towns and villages, in their parishes, with all the generations, from children to elderly people.

To support this pilgrimage, each year Brother Roger writes an open letter, often from a place of poverty where he is staying for a time (Letters from Calcutta, Warsaw, Haiti, the desert, Madras, Ethiopia, Russia . . .). This letter is then translated into 30 languages to serve as a basis for meditation in the course of the following year.

As stopping-points on this pilgrimage, Taizé has organized meetings of thousands of young people in the cathedrals and parishes of large cities: Montreal, New York, Washington, Madrid, Dublin, Lisbon, Brussels, Warsaw, East Berlin . . . . At the end of each year, a European meeting brings together several tens of thousands of young adults in a city of Eastern or Western Europe. Meetings have been held in Asian countries as well, notably in Madras, India, and the Philippines.

In 1988, on the occasion of 1,000 years of Christianity in Russia, Taizé collected money to permit one million New Testaments to be sent to Russia.

Concerned that human rights be respected, Brother Roger sometimes intervenes discreetly in situations of tension throughout the world. In the name of the young, he also makes public gestures for peace. To emphasize the symbolic nature of these gestures, he is accompanied by children from different continents, as a way of showing that he is not taking this step in his own name, as an elderly man, but in the name of those whose future is threatened. He has met with the Soviet and American ambassadors in Madrid, and with a number of heads of state. He brought to the Secretary General of the United Nations, Javier Pérez de Cuéllar, suggestions made by young people about ways the UN could create trust among nations. Mr Pérez de Cuéllar wrote, 'The pilgrimage of trust on earth organized by Taizé with young people is bringing us closer to the ideal of peace to which we all aspire'. In 1974, in London, Brother Roger was awarded the Templeton Prize, which Mother Teresa had received the previous year; the money was used to enable young people without resources from different continents to meet. The same year he was given the German Peace Prize in the presence of the West German President. In 1988, Brother Roger received the UNESCO Prize for Peace Education and in 1989, the international Karlspreis for his contribution to the construction of Europe.

Taizé thus looks for gestures and symbols that evoke, beyond present difficulties, the coming of a springtime of the Church, a Church that is rooted in the human family and is a 'land of reconciliation, sharing and simplicity'.

Other Books by Brother Roger

His Love is a Fire
Central writings with extracts from journals
Australia and New Zealand: St Paul Publications, 60 Broughton Road, Homebush, NSW 2140
Philippines: Claretian Publications, Quezon City
UK: * Geoffrey Chapman Mowbray, Stanley House, Fleets Lane, Poole BH15 3AJ
USA and Canada: The Liturgical Press, St John's Abbey, Collegeville, MN 56321

Life from Within
Prayers by Brother Roger and icons from the Church
of Reconciliation
UK: Geoffrey Chapman Mowbray
USA: Westminster Press, Louisville, KY 40202

A Heart that Trusts
Journal 1979–1981
UK: Mowbray

And Your Deserts Shall Flower
Journal 1977–1979
UK: Mowbray

By Mother Teresa of Calcutta and Brother Roger

Meditations on the Way of the Cross
India: Asian Trading Corporation, Bangalore
UK: Mowbray
USA: The Pilgrim Press, New York

Mary, Mother of Reconciliations
Australia and New Zealand: St Paul Publications
India: Daughters of St Paul, Bombay
Philippines: Claretian
UK: Mowbray
USA: Paulist Press, Mahwah, NJ

About Taizé
The Taizé Experience
Texts by Brother Roger and photographs by Vladimir
Sichov
UK: Geoffrey Chapman Mowbray
USA and Canada: The Liturgical Press

Taizé – Trust is at Hand
28-minute video-cassette. The community and the
intercontinental meetings, both in Taizé and elsewhere –
in European capitals, Madras, Brother Roger at UNESCO,
etc.
Australia and New Zealand: Rainbow Book Agencies, 134
Emmaline Street, PO Box 58, Northcote, Vic. 3070
Canada: Meakin Associates
Ireland: Veritas Publications, 7/8 Lower Abbey Street,
Dublin 1
South Africa: Century Hutchinson
UK: Geoffrey Chapman Mowbray
USA: Don Bosco Multimedia, 148 Main Street, New
Rochelle, NY 10801 (Tel: 800–342–5850)

Taizé: Trust, Forgiveness, Reconciliation
UK: Mowbray

Taizé: That Little Springtime
Video and Presenter's Guide
28-minute VHS video-cassette.
UK: Mowbray

A Pilgrimage of Trust on Earth
Colour booklet with photographs and texts about the
community and the meetings in Taizé.
UK: Mowbray

The Story of Taizé
By J. L. González Balado
The book traces the vocation of the community, from
Brother Roger's arrival, alone, in the village in eastern
France in August 1940 to the meetings which today bring
together many thousands of young adults from East and
West Europe and throughout the world.
UK: Mowbray
USA and Canada: The Liturgical Press

Music
Praying Together in Word and Song
Booklet with suggestions for prayer together, songs from
Taizé and a selection of Brother Roger's prayers.
UK: Mowbray
USA: GIA, 7407 S. Mason Avenue, Chicago, IL 60638

Music from Taizé
Two volumes. Vocal & instrumental editions.
Australia: Collins Dove Communications, PO Box 316,
Blackburn, Vic. 3130
UK: Harper Collins, London
USA and Canada: GIA

Music Cassettes

Canons et Litanies
Cantate
Alleluia (also on CD)
Resurrexit (also on CD)
Australia and New Zealand: Rainbow Book Agencies, Northcote, Vic. 3070
UK: All main stores; distribution: Redemptorist Publications, Alphonsus House, Chawton, Alton, Hants GU3 3HQ
USA and Canada: GIA

18 Songs from Taizé
UK: Mowbray

* Geoffrey Chapman Mowbray books are distributed in Australia by Canterbury Press Ltd, Unit 2, 7 Rusdale Street, Scoresby, Vic. 3179; in Canada by Meakin Associates, Unit 17, 81 Auriga Drive, Nepean, Ontario K2E 7Y5; in New Zealand: Hodder & Stoughton, PO 3858, Auckland 1; South Africa: Century Hutchinson, PO 337 Bergvlei, 20125.

The Letter from Taizé
Published every two months in fifteen languages; news from across the world, themes for group reflection, texts for meditation, prayers and daily Bible readings. Subscriptions: write to Taizé.

> The Taizé Community,
> 71250 CLUNY, France
> Telephone:
> Community: (France = 33) 85.50.30.30
>
> Meetings: (33) 85.50.30.02
>
> Telex: 800753F COTAIZE
> Fax: (33) 85.50.30.15